ISBN 978-1-334-57830-4
PIBN 10424447

1 MONTH OF
FREE
READING

at
www.ForgottenBooks.com

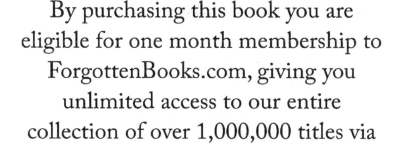

By purchasing this book you are eligible for one month membership to ForgottenBooks.com, giving you unlimited access to our entire collection of over 1,000,000 titles via our web site and mobile apps.

To claim your free month visit:
www.forgottenbooks.com/free424447

CAST OF CHARACTERS.

JUDGE CUSHING,	*Old Man.*
FRANK RAYMOND.	*Leading.*
DICK BENTON,	*Heavy.*
CHARLES MUNSON,	*Walking.*
FRED RAWLINGS.	*Character.*
JOSH SLENDER,	*First Low Comedian.*
JOE,	*Second Low Comedian.*
LENA BOSWORTH,	*Old Woman.*
ALICE RAYMOND,	*Leading.*
FANNIE STODDARD,	*Walking.*
ELLA RICE,	*Chambermaid.*
POLICEMEN, ROWDIES, MASQUERADERS, GOOD TEMPLARS, ETC., BY	*Volunteers.*

STAGE DIRECTIONS.

R. means right; L., left; R. C., right center; L. C., left center; C., center of stage; L. 1 E., left first entrance; L. U. E., left upper entrance; R. 2 E., right second entrance; L. 2 E., left second entrance.

COSTUMES.

ACT I.

SCENE I.—Light Summer clothing.

SCENE II.—*Josh*—Long linen duster; striped bed-tick pants, tight, very short, with boot-straps; broad-brimmed straw hat; striped vest; standing collar.

SCENE III.—*Joe*—White pants and vest; black coat. *Josh*—Black cut-away coat (old-fashioned), and high, bell-crowned white hat. *Other guests* in appropriate reception dresses.

ACT II.

Allie—Traveling-dress. *Frank*—Very gay walking-suit. *Fred*—Foppish costume: Wears side-whiskers; eye-glass; parts hair in middle, and sports cane.

SCENE III.—*Ladies* wear masks and black dresses.

ACT III.

SCENE I.—*Dick and Josh*—Rather shabby. *Frank*—Old, rusty, suit of black. *Allie*—Dark water-proof. *Lena*—Black.

this fast age, that lovers, or even husbands, are, as in old-fashioned times, to love and respect their sweethearts or companions? Fie! fie! You are a regular spooney, Dick. This is a spirited age. Women are becoming too independent, and men too wise or lazy, to waste their precious time and talents in making love. Love! Ha! ha! ha! It is made to order by our tailors and milliners, at our boarding-schools, and on 'change. Love is an ancient commodity, once used in cementing together hearts and hands. I'll tell you, Dick, Spalding's glue were better. Love is now considered old-fashioned—in fact, vulgar. Love is now recognized in the fashionable world as dollars and cents, houses and lands, social position. In a word, love is known, among the *elite*, as *policy*.

During latter part of above speech, CHARLIE *has crossed to* FRANK, *and motions him over to* ELLA, *whom he assists in rising, and they go down* C., *between* FANNIE *and* DICK, *just as speech is concluded.*

Frank. Now, we have caught you making love.

Fannie. Not much. Not making, but breaking.

Ella. Yes, breaking my nap. (*She beckons for* CHARLIE *to bring camp-stool to her. He does so, and she sits down and sleeps.*

Frank (*fanning* ELLA *with his hat*). Well, I trust it was a difficult task.

Fannie. Breaking naps seemed to be hard work; but love is like cat-naps, of short duration. No, no, love is like—is like (*striking dramatic attitude*)—O, by yonder hazy cloud, so pure and beautiful, I swear love is like—is like (*looking up*)—

Dick. What (*looking up as she points up*)?

Fannie (*dropping hand and turning to him quickly*). Molasses candy.

Dick. O, Lord!

Fannie. Sticks very well when it is warm; but when it grows cold, it breaks just as easy—

Charlie. (*Stumbles over one of croquet-bridges.*) As we shall our necks over these bridges. Let's remove them.

The gentlemen remove bridges, taking them off stage.

Fannie. (*Crosses to* ELLA, *and leans her mallet against her chair.*) Ella! Ella! the gentlemen are taking up the bridges!

Ella. Wait until Frank carries me across.

Fannie. O, you stupid! (ELLA *yawns.*) Yawning! (ELLA *stretches hands above head.*) Stretching! (ELLA *sneezes.*) Sneezing! Good-looking bundle of sleep, rouse yourself! (*Shakes her.*)

Ella. I am too sleepy. (*Rests head on mallet.*)

Fannie. Then, sleep! (*Pulls mallet from* ELLA'S *hand.*)

Ella. Bring back my pillow.

Dick. Charlie, look at that. (*Points to* ELLA.) Is not that a fine specimen of womanity to fall in love with?

Charlie. My dear boy, I would prefer to pay my devotions to a lady who is a little inclined to drowsiness than to fight for the affections of a girl who considers that love is like—is like—O, by yonder thunder-cloud, I swear love is like—is like—*molasses candy!* (CHAR-LIE *imitates* FANNIE'S *similar speech, burlesqueing it.*)

Frank (*looking off* R. U. E.) O, look yonder! The boys are having a spirited game of foot-ball. See, there goes a lusty drive away up through the trees. Look out! look out! (*Boy runs on from* R. U. E., *and foot-ball is tossed on. He catches it and kicks it back off* R. U. E., *and exits after it.*) Look out, there, high-kickers, the skippers are winning the game! Look sharp! Down she comes!

Ella (*yawning*). What, my pillow?

Charlie. I move we adjourn for dinner.

Ella. Bring it in here and eat it by me. It will save trouble.

Dick. Let's wait until the boys finish their game of base-ball. See there. (*Crosses to* L. U. E.) I declare, that is a sky-scraper. Run, you rascal!

Boy in base-ball costume runs on L. U. E., *and as ball comes down he catches it and exits.*

Dick. Bravo! bravo! Sam is the champion fly-catcher.

Ella. Tell him to come here and keep the flies off my nose (*brushing them away sleepily*).

Charlie. Victory for the Red-Stockings! Now, then, a song, and then for dinner.

Ella. Dinner! Is breakfast over?

Yawns and gets up. CHARLIE *crosses to her to lead her off. Other characters commence singing a lively song (music for song), and exit* L. U. E. ELLA *starts up stage, dragging stool after her. Gets to middle of stage, and sinks down on stool,* CHARLIE *trying in vain to wake her up. Other characters, having got baskets, re-enter, singing; but, seeing* ELLA, *and* CHARLES, *kneeling, kissing her hand, they all laugh.* CHARLIE *exits* L. 1 E. *Ball-players enter with others, leave bats* c., *and eat lunch* R. *and* L. *at back.*

Fannie. Well, I'm shocked! (DICK *kisses her hand. She boxes his ears.*)

Dick. So am I.

Frank. Serves you right. If there is a barbarous custom in our civilized community, it is this stupid hand-kissing.

Fannie. Perhaps you don't like it.

Frank. I do not.

Fannie. Well, I do.

Ella. So do I. (*Yawns.*)

Fannie. Were I a gentleman, I would prefer kissing your hands to venturing within saluting distance of that open mouth.

Ella. No accounting for tastes. (*Yawns.*)

Dick. Tastes! That reminds me, as I have no right to dine on any damsel's kisses, I propose we try something more substantial.

Ella. So do I. (*Yawns.*) Wake me up when my plate is heaped.

Charlie. (*Enters with basket* R. U. E.) Ella! Ella Rice! Here is this big basket, without a blessed thing in it to eat.

Ella. How stupid! I was waked up so early this morning, I knew I should forget something.

Charlie. And now I can dine on yawns.

Ella. So can I. (*Yawns.*)

Frank. I propose we divide our dinners with these unfortunates, provided Ella will perform a miracle.

Ella. I'll do it. (*Yawns.*)

Fannie. That's no miracle. Open your eyes and shut your mouth. and I'll divide my lunch.

Ella. How can I eat with my mouth shut? (*Yawns.*)

Fannie. Or open, either?

Charlie. Come, Ella, wake up, and show them that your eyes are beautiful.

Fannie. Because they are so rarely seen. (*Spreads table-cloth c.*)

Dick. Less talk, and more work! Here, Frank, you shall have the post of honor.

Charlie. Yes, sit at the head of our—our—table-cloth.

Fannie. You can sit by my side this time, since your lady-love is too shy to join us upon the morning of her wedding-day.

Frank. But the rules of society—

Fannie. O, bother society! I don't like one set of rules for the bride and another for the groom. If Allie Cushing is obliged to hide herself from her friends just because this is her wedding-day, why are you here?

Frank. To eat my dinner.

Fannie. O, I wish I was going to get married!

Ella. Me, too. (*Yawns.*) Charlie, why don't you help me down? (*Gets up.*) I can't eat, sitting so far from the festive board.

CHARLIE *kneels; but, as* ELLA *goes to sit on his knee, he sits her down on stage* L.

Fannie (*looking into basket*). O, botheration! The fruit-dish has broken! (*Takes it out and hands it to* DICK, *who kneels at her* R. *He groans,* CHARLIE *gives shrill whistle,* ELLA *yawns, and* FRANK *laughs. This business is repeated every time* FANNIE *takes any thing from basket. The dishes, etc., should be smeared over to imitate dirt.*) I declare! In our horse-racing, one of the champagne-bottles has burst. (*Repeat business explained above.*) Dear! dear! The pie-plate has smashed (*hands it to* CHARLIE. *Repeat business*), and the pickles are swimming in the custard. (*Gives pickle to* ELLA. *Repeat business.*) O, tormentation! The jelly-flasks have upset, and the pound-cake is floating in the pudding-gravy. (*Hands* FRANK *a pound-cake, and repeat business.*) Did you ever see such a mess of mystery? O, such a fearful conglomeration! (*Rises.*)

Frank. Good! I like hash. (*Rises.*)

Charlie. Yes, private hash, and not boarding-house confidence games. But champagne and pickles—bah! I prefer to mix my own liquors. (*Rises.*)

Dick. Well, it's plain we can eat none of this mince pie and sausage. (*Rises.*)

Ella. Why not? It would save us all so much trouble.

Fannie. How so, Sleepy?

Ella. It's already chawed. Well, if I can't get any dinner, I'll take my regular nap. (*She takes the basket for pillow, and leans head upon it and sleeps.*)

Dick. Let's unbasket the wine, and drown sorrow in a glass of claret.

Fannie. You had better wait until after dessert.

Dick. We have already deserted (*aside*) that dinner.

CHARLIE *removes cloth; with things in it, from stage.*

Fannie. You *gentlemen* had better wait about your drinking until the *ladies* withdraw.

Ella. The ladies are too sleepy to withdraw. I have been cheated out of my dinner and out of my nap, and now, fashion or not, I am dry.

Charlie. Ella, there is a spring of water yonder (*points* R. 2 E.) I will bring you a glass of water.

Frank (*to Charlie*). Give me the glass. You remain and keep the little dear awake, while I fetch it a drink. (*Exit* R, 2 E.)

Dick. Ha! ha! ha! That was well played. Water! He made that an excuse to avoid drinking with us. Gentlemen, have some wine? (DICK *has basket of wine, and fills glasses, which he hands to others, who come down.*)

Fannie. They say he is a Good Templar.

Charlie. No, I think not; but I believe his name has been proposed as a member of ——— Lodge.

Dick. Well, here is my opinion of ——— Lodge. I believe these Sons of Temperance, Templars of Honor, Young Templars, and Good Templars are humbugs. But here is to their success. (*Drinks swallow of wine from glass.* ELLA *yawns, and all laugh.*)

Charlie. See here, Dick Benton, I am not a Good Templar, but I am a friend of temperance, and I consider you are using too strong language.

Dick. Yes, my dear boy, but it's a strong subject. I believe we have cringed and fawned to these temperance quackers quite long enough. I am for the greatest good to the greatest number; and, so long as the majority are opposed to this subject of temperance, I say let the minority—

Fannie. Grin and bear it.

ELLA *yawns, and all laugh.*

Dick. I say the minority have no right to be eternally hammering away upon this same old subject—Temperance (*drinks*)! *Temperance* (*drinks*)! TEMPERANCE (*drinks*)!

Charlie. You seem to consider it a dry subject.

ELLA *yawns, and all laugh.*

Dick. And then these secret societies—who knows any thing about them? They meet with closed doors, and the outer world is uninformed regarding their acts. Why don't the Churches make secret societies of their religious organizations? Were these Good Templars so mighty solicitous for public morality, why do n't they throw open their doors and say to the unfortunate, Come in and examine our public works of reformation? For my part, I am opposed to these Good Templars.

Frank. (*Enters with glass of water* R. 1 E.) So I see. (ELLA *yawns, and others laugh.* FRANK *crosses to* CHARLIE.) Charlie, I had a hot walk, but it was an easier task than keeping that bundle of morphine's eyes open. (*All laugh.* ELLA *yawns.*)

Fannie. Or her mouth closed. Mr. Benton, I will trouble you for another taste of that superb wine. (DICK *fills her glass.*)

Charlie. Ella! Ella! (*Crosses, and shakes her violently. She snores. All laugh.*) Ella! Ella Rice! Fire! thieves! murder! (*Screaming. Then says, softly:*) Here's something good to drink.

ELLA *jumps up quickly, and all laugh. She goes to take glass.*

Ella. O, dear! Wake me up to drink nothing but water! Thank you, sir. I am not half as thirsty as I am sleepy, for I have just been drinking wine.

Charlie. Ella, was that right? Knowing my principles of total abstinence, you should have too much respect to drink even a glass of wine in my presence.

Ella. O, do n't preach! It always makes me sleepy. Remember we are not married yet—this is but an engagement ring. I drank what I liked best, and intend to drink more.

Charlie (*offering glass*). Pure cold water, Ella.

Ella. I declare! That puritanic whine makes me yawn. (*She goes to stretch her hands out, when she accidentally drops ring into glass of water.*) O, my beautiful diamond ring will be ruined by that horrid water!

Charlie. A diamond which loses its brilliancy by a cup of pure water is no befitting emblem of my affection. (*Carelessly tosses water and ring over his shoulder.*)

Fannie. Thus are modern engagements made and broken.

Ella. (*Sits on stool* L. 2 E.) All on account of a glass of wine. Well, I guess I 'll not break my heart (*yawns*), or my nap, either. (*Sleeps.*)

Frank. Charlie, my dear fellow, allow me to congratulate you. (*Crosses to Charlie* R. C.)

Dick (*coming up* R. C.) I say, Charlie, we will all drink to your better success next time. Eh? Fannie?

Fannie. No, I won't drink any more. He is n't worth the compliment. Get mad and break his engagement because a young lady dares assert her rights!

Ella. Or any other man.

Dick. Here, Frank, is your glass of wine, untasted. (*Offers him one.*)

Frank. Thank you, I am not thirsty.

Dick. Come, come, now, no quibbling. It 's cowardly to refuse, when asked to drink.

Frank. Yes, it is cowardly, and I 'll never do it again so long as I live.

Dick. Good! good! Let's drink to that sentiment. It is cowardly to refuse. (*All raise glasses.*)

Frank. Cowardly for a man—a self-reliant, honorable man—to shrink from avowing his principles, and hide away behind such cowardly excuses (*all lower glasses*) as, No, thank you, I am not thirsty; or, I never drink in public!, Why is it necessary for a temperance man to thus disgrace himself by sneaking behind such shabby lies? Were you to say to me, Let's go lie, steal, or murder, would the rules of etiquette require me, as a gentleman, to answer, politely, Pray excuse me? No! I'd assert my manhood by a blow straight from the shoulder—meet the request to drink as I will hereafter!

Dick. Very well, then, let's take a drink.

Frank. No.

Dick. Why not?

Frank. I never drink.

Dick. Just this once. (*Offers glass.*)

Frank. Not one single drop.

Dick. O, come, now, don't get sulky. Drink this social glass with me. (*Offers it.*)

Frank. Sir, you insult me. (*He haughtily dashes* DICK'S *hand and glass away.*)

Dick. See here, Frank Raymond, we want none of your temperance speeches here. You are putting on too much style to suit this crowd. Perhaps you think yourself too good to drink a glass of wine with me?

Frank. Yes, sir, you or any other man.

Dick. (*Goes down* C. FRANK *goes up.*) See here, boys. (*They all go down except* FRANK. CHARLIE *crosses to* ELLA *and* FANNIE L.) Frank Raymond swears he is too good to drink a social glass with us. Now, I say he shall drink; and, if not peaceably, then we will make him.

Omnes. Yes! yes! Make him drink! (*Let every gentleman on stage, except* FRANK *and* CHARLIE, *say this.*)

Frank. Gentlemen, you would not forget ladies' presence, and resort to acts of violence.

Dick. Well, we will, my fine fellow. You are just coward enough to sneak behind the ladies. Here, take this glass of wine. (*Goes up* C.)

Frank. Never! (*Music—a hurry till change.*)

Dick. (*Goes down* C. *to crowd.*) Seize him, and I will pour it down his throat, the stubborn fool. (*Let the crowd advance a step or two, as though they would seize him.*)

Frank. Gentlemen, my temperance principles are as dear to me as honor, and I will defend them with my life!

PICTURE—FRANK *seizes ball-bat, which he holds over head in act of striking.* ELLA *rises, and* CHARLIE *raises camp-chair as though to attack crowd.* ELLA *clings to his arm.* FANNIE *shakes her fist at* DICK, *who stands near* FRANK, *as though intimidated. The crowd all take position of attack, and every body stands perfectly still until scene is closed in. Be careful to keep center of stage in front of* FRANK *clear of people.*

SCENE II.—*Wood in one. Noise and confusion heard off* L. 1 E.

Josh Slender (*outside*). Whoa! whoa! Gee! whoa! haw! Gee! Whoa! (*He leaps as far onto stage as possible, and falls. His velocipede is pushed on from off stage, just far enough to show front wheel.*) There, I thought you would stop somewhere. Whoa, now, don't kick! (*Sits up.*) Wall, chaw me into sassengers if that ain't the allfiredest thing to stop I ever started. (*Sees velocipede. Moves off* R., *without getting up.*) Whoa, there! Lay still, or I'll knock a wheel plum off! (CHARLIE MUNSON *laughs off* L. 1 E.) Here, you Tom Frazier, come and see if I am all here. I feel as though I'd been jerked by a mile-a-minute steam-plow over forty acres of stump pasture. (*Gets up.*) Whoa, there! Stop friskin' your tail! Blast the tarnal thing! If you ever catch me trying tew break a velocipeder tew ride, you can call my old mother a Dutchman, by chowder! Ridin' them is wus than breakin' a yoke of four-year-old muley bulls. I'd rather ride a three-legged blind mule, bare-backed, with a chestnut-burr under his fly-switcher. Whoa, there, or I'll spring a linch-pin! I was out looking after Judge Cushing's cows, and came by where a lot of fellows was picker-nicking, up there on the hill. Tom Frazier and Bill Poole got me onto this tarnal critter, told me to hang on, and down the hill I come like forty wild-cats—jilty! jolty! over stones and into ruts!—barked my shins against an old stump!—wobble and tumble!—knocked my head against an old limb, shied that big rock, chucked up against that blasted tree, and stopped—stopped before I had time to get off, and landed me out here about forty feet, ker-bump!

Charlie Munson. (*Enters* L. 1 E.) Try it again.

Josh. Try the d—ickens! Mister Munson, dew you think I'm a nateral born fool, or had all my senses shook out of me? (CHARLIE *goes up to velocipede.*) Wall, by jingo, if he ain't bolder than dad's old cosset sheep! Now, I'd rather play with a double-geared chain of greased lightning than fool round another of these infernal patent machines.

Charlie. Are you afraid of it, Josh?

Josh. No sir-ee bob, horse and wagon! (CHARLIE *starts it toward him.*) But I don't hanker after it any closer. Keep the pesky thing away, or I'll kick a wheel plum off! I will, by ginger!

Charlie. Now, just watch me make it zip. (*Exits with velocipede* L. 1 E.)

Josh. Jess so! There you go onto your nose. Say, Mister Munson, don't try to ride that pesky thing back up-hill, or it will get its back up, and kick up sideways. Gosh darn your velocipeders!

Dick Benton. (*Enters* L. 1 E.) Halloo, Josh, what's the matter?

Josh. Velocipeders.

Dick. You look down-in-the-mouth.

Josh. Dew tell! Wall, I looked down somewhere else, a minute ago. Say, Mister Benton, did you ever slide down the Green Mountings on a hemlock plank, with all the slivers sticking the wrong way?

Dick. Never had that pleasure. It must give one a queer sensation.

Josh. Sensation ain't no name tew compare with ridin' that velocipeder down that hill.

Dick. Did it run hard?

Josh. Hard? No, it run too easy; but it stopped hard.

Dick. Josh, I believe you are a good, sensible fellow.

Josh. Wall, I used tew flatter myself that way; but the last ten minutes' experience has shook all such conceit clean out of me.

Dick. Have you found work yet?

Josh. Not a lick, only off jobs.

Dick. See here, Josh, how would you like to tend saloon?

Josh. Say—say—say it again, slow. Sa-loon. Is that French for velocipeders?

Dick. No, no. Practice at the bar.

Josh. Study law?

Dick. Not much. Stand behind the bar of a retail liquor-saloon.

Josh. A whisky-shop? What! Me, Josh Slender, turn gin-peddler? No, Mister Benton. I'm hard-up—hain't got a sixpence in my trousers pockets; lost my jack-knife, too; hain't had a square meal in a week, and don't know when the next one is comin' round but I promised my old marm, when I left her tew hum in Vermont, that I'd starve, or 'arn an honest livin'.

Dick. Well?

Josh. Wall, it ain't honest tew lie?

Dick. No, indeed.

Josh. Jess so. Nor 't ain't honest tew steal?

Dick. Certainly not.

Josh. Exactly. Nor 't aint honest tew murder?

Dick. What are you driving at? No, sir, it is neither honest to lie, steal, nor murder.

Josh. Wall, Mister Benton, selling liquor embraces all of them modern accomplishments. Marm told me, when I come off West—"Josh," says she, "Joshua, my son, Josephus, don't drink licker. It's a bad habit. It's nasty. It's wuss nor chawin' terbacker, layin' on your back with the night-mare.

Dick. O, your mother was no doubt a good, old-fashioned dame, who brought you up in strict conformity to the old blue-laws.

Josh. Yes, but old blue-laws are better than old blue-devils. Selling liquor ain't not respectable.

Dick. Why look at me? Ain't I respectable?

Josh. Wall, you wear good cloaths. Yes, you—you look kinder about half-way decent.

Dick. Yet I am proprietor of a saloon.

Josh. Yes, but you want tew hire me tew dew all the dirty work.

Dick. O, no. I sell liquor myself, sometimes. Somebody must sell, and why should I shrink from a licensed occupation which will support me and mine? I am the proprietor of a grand palace concert saloon, where all the aristocracy of the city, even including Judge Cushing, take their drams.

Josh. Does Judge Cushing drink at your bar?

Dick. Certainly, (*aside*) in a horn. (*Aloud.*) He is my personal, for I am his political friend.

Josh. Wall, Mister Benton, I don't know much about you; but I do know that Judge Cushing is a Church-member, and I ain't afraid but what he is O. K. I am just out looking after the judge's cows.

They're going to have a wedding up there to-night, and I s'pose they
want a little 'sweet milk for the tea-total bridegroom. I've about
made up my mind that my old marm is a little old-fashioned. Gosh-
ashun! I've heard her say so more 'n a billion times! Wall, I'll just
drive up the judge's critters, and ask him if selling liquor is just the
cheese out West here; and, if he says it am, I'll get behind your bar
double-quick (DICK *starts to exit* L. 1 E.)—provided, now, remember,
I'm not to taste of your customers' liquors when mixing a gin-sling,
or to wheel your staggering visitors home on a velocipeder. (DICK
exits L. 1 E. JOSH *exits* R. 1 E. *Lively music till scenes changed.*)

SCENE III.—*Full stage. Interior folding doors. Represents* JUDGE
CUSHING'S *parlor. Table stands* R. U. E., *with cakes and wine.
Glasses filled half-full. Enough for all guests. Sofa* R. *and* L.,
with few nice chairs. A small stand L. U. E., *with flowers.*

Judge Cushing. (*Enters* C., *shaking hands with* FRED RAWLINGS.)
My dear boy, I am delighted to welcome you back from your long
journey.
Fred Rawlings. Aw, weally, thank you—aw. I am extwemely
wejoiced that I have weturned in time to congwatulate you upon
this happy mawwiage.
Judge. Thank you. Frank and Allie will soon be here. I left
them at the church-door, and hastened home to see that all was
in readiness for the reception. Bless my soul! I have walked so
fast that I have set my nerves in a great flurry.
Fred. Aw, weally, you have, by jove! So Allie is mawwied. I
can scarcely wealize that my little playmate is Fwank Waymond's
wife. They are to sail for Euwope soon?
Judge. They leave for New York in an hour and a half. Bless
me, how nervous I am getting! From New York they sail for
Europe, in a few days. O, my nerves! A few of their personal
friends will accompany them here from church. A little cake-eat-
ing, lots of wine-drinking; a few tears, lots of laughter, and then
farewell to the old home. Heaven make their new one as happy!
Fred. Amen, by Jove! I twust it will be. Fwank is a genewous
fellow, and his gweat wealth will only be squandered to surround
his bwide with luxuries abounding in the home of her childhood.
I hope they will live a thousand years—I do, by Jove!

JOSH *knocks very loud* L. 1 E.

Judge. Bless my nervous soul! What's that? Who in the
world has straggled into the hall, and knocks at my parlor door
like a drunken peddler? Some fool! (FRED *sits up stage. Reads
paper.*)
Josh. (*Enters* L. 1 E., *bowing and scraping.*) Yes, sir. Jess so,
sir. Exactly, sir. It's me, sir. I've found the cow.
Judge. Well, booby, do you wish to bring her into my parlor.
Josh. Yes, sir. Jess so, sir. Exactly, sir. Yes, sir, if you want
her handy. (*Going out* L. 1 E., *bowing, etc.*)

Judge. Stop! Tell me, Josh, where in the world did you drop from?

Josh. From a' velocipede, sir. Yes, sir. Now, Jedge, I'll not entertain you but two shakes of a lamb's tail. You are a lawyer?

Judge. I was formerly, (*aside*) Heaven forgive me!

Josh. Jess so, jedge. Exactly, sir. Yes, sir. Are you old-fashioned?

Judge. Old-fashioned? O, how my nerves jump! Old-fashioned! No, sir!

Josh. Jess so, jedge. Exactly, sir. Yes, sir. I do n't know why I 'm glad, but somehow I kinder am. (*Aside.*) O, my, I 've put my foot in it now. (*Aloud.*) Jedge, one more question: Are you respectable?

Judge. Zounds! you scoundrel! (*shaking cane at* JOSH, *who bows and scrapes rapidly.*) Do you wish to insult me? O, my nerves! Respectable! You—you—you—

Josh. Jess so, jedge. No offense. I forgive you. (*Aside.*) Now I 've put t' other foot in it wuss than ever. It won't do to ax him about the Benton whisky speculation now. (*Aloud.*) Jedge, I got my questions a little mixed. I was intending to ask, Do you consider, or do you consider—

Judge. Consider what (*shaking cane*)?

Josh. Velocipeders respectable?

JOSH *retires up stage, wiping his face with large red handkerchief. Does not see* FRED *sitting* L., *and stumbles over his feet just as* JOE *enters* C. JOSH *runs against him, and then, in confusion, backs down stage until he runs against* JUDGE, *who seats him violently on sofa* R. JOE *does not advance upon stage, but speaks in door* C.

Joe. Mas'r Cushing, dat extra white nigga what you 'gaged to 'sist dis cullud gen'leman in totin' 'roun' de freshments hain't yet 'ribed.

Judge. Bless my soul! Every thing conspires to shock my nerves to-day (*going up to table*).

Josh. Jess so, jedge.

Judge. I have it. (*Raises glass of wine.*) Josh, do you think—

Josh. No, sir, I never drink.

Judge. Ha! ha! ha! (*jumps.*) O, that twinge of my gout! Do you *think*—

Josh. Very seldom.

Judge. Could you assist that good-looking servant of mine?

Joe. Dat's me. Golly!

Judge. Can you help him pass the liquor?

Josh (*jumps up*). Wall, chaw me inter mince pies if that wa' n't persactly the p'int I cum tew ax yew about.

Judge. All right. Take your position, and, above all things else, do n't get nervous. (*Exit* C.)

Fred. Waitah!

JOE *starts toward* FRED, *then stops and motions* JOSH *to answer the call.* JOSH *raises fist as though to knock* JOE *down.*

Fred. Waitah! (JOE *goes to him.*)
Joe. Sah!

FRED. Wemove this papah, and.place it with my beavah.

JOE. Yes, sah. (*Takes paper and exits* c.)

FRED. Wait—(*beckoning to* JOSH.)

JOSH. Wait—(*shaking his fist.*)

FRED. Ah!

JOSH. The niggah is now heah.' (*Enter* JOE c.)

FRED. Waitah!

JOE. Yes, sah.

FRED. A glass of clawet to wemove the dust of twavel.

JOE hands FRED *glass of wine.*

JOSH. Waitah! '(*imitating* FRED.)

JOE. Get out!

JOSH. A glass of watah to wemove this potatah, so I will not stam-mah in this bad mannah.

FRED. (*Hands glass to* JOE, *puts up eye-glass, and crosses toward* JOSH.) Aw, weally, me faih-haiwed boy, you are shawp, you are, upon my honah; but, by jove, don't ask an old man of uppah fen-dom if he is—aw—wespectable.

JOSH. Wall, stranger, I don't have tew wear goggles tew make out that there ain't not any use in askin' you that question.

FRED. Take youw place at the side-boawd, and less impudence. (*Exits* c.)

JOSH. Wall, by jingo! I've heard tell of buck-boards, and teter-boards, boardin' 'round, and all aboard; but I swear, old black-board, (*to* JOE) what and where is a side-board? (JOE *points to table, behind which he stands, arranging glasses.*) Wall; gosh durn my pewter buttons if Judge Cushing hain't got a private whisky-shop in his spare room. This must be what they call new fashions. Wall, I reckon if it's right tew wait on Judge Cushing's guests tew licker in his parlor, it must be correct tew help Dick Benton's visitors at his saloon, where drinking liquor belongs. I see I've been brought up tew far toward the rising sun. I'm green. I'm too allfired old-fashioned for the West; but I'll show that grinnin' burlesque on American citizenship that I know a thing or two about "wespectable" society. (JOSH *fixes his hat firmly on his head, takes out handker-chief, and blows his nose violently.*) Waitah, five cents worth of rum!

JOE. G'way from heah, white trash! Guess you don't know whar you is, and who you's sultin', orderin' *rum.*

JOSH. (*Aside.*) I knew I'd surprise him with my knowledge of fashionable drinks. I'd order a lemonade or a ginger pop, only I want he should think I'm used tew these fashionable lickers. I'll raise him a cent. (*Swaggers up to counter with hat on side of head.*) Give us six cents worth of *brandy.*

JOE. (*Aside.*) 'Spec' dat green-horn's drunk. Dese poor white trash don't know 'nuff to drink when dey's dry. (*Aloud.*). Do you think you is in —— saloon, orderin' brandy?

JOSH. (*Aside.*) My knowledge of fashionable beverages makes that benighted African look pale. I'll go it a little stronger. (*Puts hat on back of head. Thrusts hands into pants-pockets.*) Seven cents worth of *whisky.*

JOE. See heah, my friend. (*Comes out and lays hand on* JOSH's *shoulder.*)

JOSH. Look here, Africa, take them cotton-pickers off of my good cloaths immejiate, if not sooner. (JOE *removes hand.* JOSH *brushes dirt from shoulder.*)

JOE. O, I ain't proud. I ain't 'shamed ob your ole close. (*Locks arms with* JOSH, *and come down* c.)

JOSH. See here, nigger! (*quickly taking attitude of attack.*)

JOE. Nigga'? Who you callin' nigga'? (JOSH *approaches, as though to strike.*) Look out, dar, white man, don't you struck dis chile, or he'll hab you up 'fore Mayor —— for tryin' to make me salt an' butter you. Now, I want to tole you something! You is ole-fashioned. (JOSH *threatening to strike.*) Steddy, dar, on de right! You is green, and 'dat's wuss dàn bein' black. (JOSH *threatens.*) Go slow, dar, Yank, cos' you's a fool. (JOSH *knocks him down. Let* JOE *fall heavily, and* JOSH *stand over him, with foot raised, as though to kick him.* JOE *sits up, rubbing his head.*) Who frowed dat last brick fust? Golly! dat was a stunner! See heah, you's too careless, boss—you is, suah. (*Gets up.*) Don't be skeered. I won't hurt you. (*Crawls away from* JOSH, *and gets up.*) Don't be 'fraid. I wouldn't struck you more dan I would my own mudder, if I'd ebber had one. (JOSH *advances with raised hand,* JOE *escaping.*) Don't 'larm yourself. I's as gentle as a lamb.

JOSH. Yes, 'cos I lammed you.

JOE. Dese lickers you mention are not known in de 'ristocratic 'cabulary. Dey nebber 'pear on de side-board or in a gen'leman's parlor; but whenebber you find wine and champagne up-stairs, dere's brandy and whisky in de cellar, for de old buffers. Allus drink light lickers in ladies' presence—'cos why, dat's fashionable. (*Retires behind table* R.)

JOSH. (*Aside.*) Expect that shade of Ethiopia knows more 'bout fashionable spirits than I do; but I'll try again. (*Takes off hat and buttons up coat, and orders pompously, retiring behind table* R. *as guests enter.*) Give us ten cents worth of gin and molasses.

Lively music. JUDGE CUSHING *enters* C., *bowing to guests as they enter.* MUNSON *and* FANNIE *enter* C., *arm-in-arm, and take sofa* R. BENTON *and* ELLA *follow, and take sofa* L. RAWLINGS *and lady, and gent and lady, enter and go* R. *and* L., *and others, if stage is large.* JOE *takes one waiter, and* JOSH *the other, with half-filled glasses on each, and pass to guests, then retire behind table.*

CHARLIE. Fannie, my dear girl, do you think that Mr. Benton and Miss Rice will ever become husband and wife.

FANNIE. Really, Mr. Munson, I would not have any such needless fears, for the stupid thing can't keep awake long enough for him to propose.

ELLA. Mr. Benton, are you engaged?

DICK. Well, really, my dear girl—(*Rises, confused.*)

ELLA. Yes or no. Are you engaged?

DICK. (*Aside.*) Jerusalem! She is going to propose. (*Aloud.*) No.

ELLA. Then, if you love me—

DICK. Yes! yes! (*Kneels, taking her hand.*)

ELLA (*turning away languidly*). Wake me up when the bridegroom comes. (*Yawns, and, dropping head on sofa-arm, sleeps. Dick jumps up quickly. During this speech JOE has taken his place in c. door, and now announces. All guests rise and bow as bride and groom enter.*)

JOE. Mr. and Mrs. Frank Raymond.

Lively music. JOE *exits* c. FRANK *and* ALLIE *enter* c. *door and stand* c., JUDGE *at their* L. FRED *comes up* R. ALLIE *stands on* FRANK'S L.

FRED. Fwank, my deah fellow, allow me to be the first to offer my vewy best. May youh wedded life be an eternity of happiness! Now, Allie, I claim but one pwivilege, to-night. It's mine by a seniowity of fwiendship. I wish to offah the congwatulatowy toast, "To the bwide!"

EVERY BODY. To the bride! (*raising glasses high.* JUDGE *crosses to* DICK.)

FRANK. Thank you, sir. (*Turns to* JOSH.) A glass of water for me. (*Guests lower glasses.*)

JOSH. Don't water your liquor. It's not fashionable.

FRED. Cowwect. We want the puah bevewage to-night. Happiness and long life to the bwide! (*Raises glass.*)

FRANK. Ah, Fred, do not mar that happiness by proposing a toast which I see must be drank in wine.

JUDGE *crosses back to* ALLIE.

JUDGE. Eh? What's that?

FRED. Fwank, don't be an old fogy. You awe suwwounded by the votawies of fashion. Now, don't be too wadical on youh old hobby, tempewance.

FRANK. Say, rather, too neglectful of my principles of total abstinence.

FRED. But you will suwely dwink this once. See, youh obstinacy is attwacting the attention of youh guests. Dwink youh bwidal toast.

FRANK. No, sir. It is against my principles.

JUDGE. Principles be—hanged! O, my nerves! What have principles to do with a newly married man? Do you realize where you are, sir?

FRANK. Yes, but these surroundings would almost lead me to believe that I was *not* in a *gentleman's* parlor.

JUDGE (*going all about stage in his fury*). Zounds! how nervous I am getting! Are you aware, sir, that you are offering a gross and unpardonable insult to my daughter, your wife?

FRANK. It would be a greater insult were I to so far forget her purity as to drink intoxicating liquor in presence of the only woman I ever loved.

JUDGE. What will people say?

FRANK. Who cares what they say? O, sir, do not try to frighten me into doing wrong by this bug-bear of fashionable tattle! Once, and for the last time, I will only drink the toast in cold water.

JOSH. (*Comes out to* FRANK'S R.) You're old-fashioned. Beg pardon, sir. (*Bows.*) You're green. (*Scrapes.*) Excuse me, sir You're not respectable.

JUDGE. Silence, fool!

JOSH. Jess so, jedge. Yes, sir. Exactly, sir. (*Exits* R. 2 E.)

JUDGE (*crossing and recrossing stage as he speaks*). Frank Raymond, don't get excited. Keep cool, or you'll make me nervous; and I would not welcome you as my son-in-law beneath this roof only in anger, to bid you leave it forever. (*Very angry and excited.*) Now, don't fly into a passion. Don't get nervous. Pattern after me; for, by the eternal, if you dare thus publicly to bring disgrace upon me and mine, the house you insult shall no longer be your home!

ALLIE. (*Goes and lays hand on his shoulder.*) O, father!

JUDGE. (*Throws off her hand angrily.*) Don't father me, madam. Teach your husband to show me proper respect, or do not dare to insult me by the name of father. (*Exits in rage* C.)

ALLIE. Frank, I am very sorry. Kind friends, will you excuse me. (*Exit* C.)

CHARLES. (*Crosses to* FRANK R.) Frank, as your friend, let me urge you. I am opposed to drinking intoxicating liquors as a beverage, but upon this occasion I would yield a little. See, you are surrounded by the votaries of fashion.

FRANK. My friends, none can regret this unfortunate termination of our bridal festivities more profoundly than myself. I am grieved that you surround me here, upon my wedding night, holding in your good right hands, which I so oft have pressed in friendship, that which should reflect its own blush of shame to every honest face. Raise your glasses higher, still higher, and let the red wine sparkle in its beauty. Now, pause (*all glasses held high*) and reflect. Thus, even thus, in our pleasant homes, in our fashionable parlors, is the first step taken in the drunkard's career. (*Lower glasses.*) It is a shame, a burning, blasting shame, that these fashionable, aristocratic home manufactories of drunkards are not frowned upon by public sentiment, and that, even at open house on New Year's day, any lady should convert reception-rooms into a recruiting station for King Alcohol!

CHARLES. Frank! Frank! Are you mad? Think what you are saying. Here, take my glass. (FRANK *does so.*) Now, drink.

FRANK. No, sir. Never!

CHARLES. (*Aside.*) Well, pretend you drink.

FRANK. And act a lie?

CHARLES. For my sake.

ALLIE *and* JUDGE *enter* C.

FRANK. Charles Munson, you have known me from childhood. You know that at a broken-hearted mother's death-bed, I kneeled down upon the floor beside the remains of my murdered father, and swore by my hopes of heaven I would never drink that which killed him. You know that I have never violated that oath—never have drunk the first drop of intoxicating liquor. If I drink this glass of wine, I may become a drunkard. If I do, Charles Munson, at the last great day will you stand beside me then as now, and, looking up into my mother's sainted face, even at the throne of God, will you be responsible for the first glass?

CHARLIE. (*After a moment's pause, pushes away glass from* FRANK's *lips.*) No I dare not.

ALLIE. (*Steps forward to* FRANK *and takes his glass.*) *I dare! Drink!* I know that my love for you and yours for me will shield you from over-indulgence. I take the responsibility. Drink! It is our bridal toast. Frank, take it, for my sake. Husband, if you love me, drink!

ALLIE *raises the glass to his lips. He drinks. Other guests stand in sorrow, without drinking.* BENTON *is smiling and nodding his head at the* JUDGE, *who is rubbing his hands in high glee.* TABLEAU. SLOW CURTAIN.

ACT II.

SCENE I.—*Same as* ACT I, SCENE III. *One sofa* L. 2 E. *Two chairs* R. 2 E. *Small stand* L. C. *Table* R. U. E. *Server, with half-dozen half-filled glasses, off stage at back. Lively music at curtain.*

JUDGE. (*Enters* C., *shaking hands with* FRANK, *who is very lively in speech and action.*) My dear boy, I am glad you have returned in safety.

FRANK. Yes, safe and sound. (*They go down* R. C.)

CHARLES. (*Enters with* ALLIE C.) Allie, I congratulate you upon the safety with which you have accomplished your long journey. (*They sit upon sofa.*)

ALLIE. Thank you, Cousin Charlie, we have had a splendid time.

FRANK. You bet! A jolly old time! Here, Joe!

JOE. (*Enters* C.) Hello!

FRANK. Some catawba.

JOE. What-aw-by?

FRANK. Catawba, fool!

JOE. Golly! Is dat furrin? 'Fore goodness, Mas'r Frank, I'se dun forgot what kind ob licker catawby fool is.

FRANK. Sir!

JOE. Yes, sir. (JOE *going out* C.)

FRANK. Here, Joe!

JOE. Hello! (*Returns.*)

FRANK. Some port.

JOE. Yes, sah. (*Going.*)

FRANK. Here, Joe!

JOE (*very loud*). Hello!

FRANK. Some claret.

JOE. Yes, sah. (*Going.*)

FRANK. Here, Joe!

JOE (*faintly, as though exhausted*). Hello!

FRANK. Nothing more.

JOE (*counting on fingers, aside*). Catawby fool—claret—port—nothing more. Golly! 'Spec' I'd better bring him 'alf-and'alf. (*Exit* c.)

FRANK. Father, do you remember, six months ago to-night, how mad you got, because I refused to drink a glass of wine? You threatened to kick me out if I would n't drink; and I swore I'd never touch, taste, nor handle the damnable poison. Ha! ha! ha! And do you remember, Allie, you held the glass to my lips then? Now, I can help myself.

Enter JOE c., *with glasses on waiter. He goes to table* L. *and sets them down.*

JOE. Dat's right, help yourself. (*Exit quickly* c. FRANK *drinks*.)

JUDGE. I say, Frank. Ha! ha! ha! Bless my soul, I'm getting nervous again. Ain't you getting a little too fast?

FRANK. Fast? fast? Why, I think I am blamed slow, when you think what good teachers I've had. Eh? Allie? (*Punches* JUDGE *in ribs, and drinks swallow.*)

JUDGE. Ha! ha! ha! O, dear, my nerves are getting all unstrung. Frank, you rascal, ain't you going it a little—just a leetle too strong?

FRANK. Strong? (*Drinks.*) Strong? (*Drinks.*) Bah! This is only sweetened water. I am no longer a baby drunkard, that you need thus nurse my appetite. I am a full-grown, manly drunkard. and crave *brandy.*

JUDGE. Brandy! O, my nerves!

FRANK. O, I beg your pardon. I forgot that I was in a parlor where brandy was considered vulgar. Never mind. Come up with me to Dick Benton's Gem Saloon to-night, and then you'll see me pop 'em off. (*Slaps* JUDGE *on shoulder, hard. He coughs.*) You'll never have cause to blush for me again, old man.

JUDGE. Old man! Nonsense! Be careful of that temper, sir. Keep cool, now, and no bullying. You are getting too careless in the use of the wine-glass. You drink too often.

FRANK. Often? (*Drinks.*) Often? (*Drinks.*) Why, this is but a fashionable thimble measure—only half a swallow.

JUDGE. Now, hark ye, Frank, are you going to make a drunkard of yourself?

FRANK. Make a drunkard of myself? O, no. (*Drinks.*) But my friends will, unless I look sharp.

JUDGE. Yes, and look mighty sharp, too; for, if you go to getting drunk and making a beast of yourself, the house you insult shall no longer be your home.

ALLIE. (*Crosses and lays hand on his shoulder.*) O, father!

CHARLES *rises.*

JUDGE. Do n't father me, madam! Teach your *husband* to show me proper respect, or do not insult *me* with the name of *father!* (*Exit* c.)

ALLIE. Frank Raymond, I am ashamed of you! (*Exit* c.)

FRANK (*his manner now more serious, aside*). Strange! strange!
Those were the very words he used six months ago, in this room,
when I refused to drink; and now that I do drink, just to please
him and Allie, he gets mad and goes to bullying. (*Goes up to table
and pours out glass of liquor. Aloud.*) Charlie, old pard, people
are constantly growling about mothers-in-law; but I say, most em-
phatically, confound my wife's father!

CHARLIE. Frank, come and sit down. I wish to talk to you. (*He
has placed two chairs down* C.)

FRANK. Yes, talk to me like a father or a Dutch uncle, but not like
a father-in-law. (*Coming down, with glass and bottle.*)

CHARLIE. Frank, I am afraid you are going to the devil.

FRANK. I *know* I am, and I've got through tickets. (*Holds up
bottle and glass, and sits* L.)

CHARLIE. Will you listen to reason? (*Sits in chair* R.)

FRANK. Reason! Look around. See this bottle and glass; see all
these surroundings, and blush to say reason to me.

CHARLIE. What do you think of these Good Templars?

FRANK. (*Quickly.*) They are bricks. (*Drinks.*)

CHARLIE. Now, be serious. I am going to join them.

FRANK. Bravo! Allow me to congratulate you; but excuse my
shaking on it. (*He has bottle in one hand, and glass in the other.
As he raises glass to drink,* CHARLES *takes it from him and puts it
on stage at* R. *of his chair.* FRANK *goes to drink from bottle, but,*
CHARLIE *trying to take it,* FRANK *puts it on stage* L.) Yes, you had
better join these meddling Good Templars, if you are not man
enough to mind your own business.

CHARLIE. Do not be angry, Frank. I am not man enough to resist
my appetite; and when I remember how you had lived all your life
a teetotaler, then yielded to temptation, and are now floating down
the mad current to destruction, I tremble for my own safety, and
mean to take every precaution against becoming a drunkard.

FRANK. All right, old boy; and let me tell you, be careful of the
first glass. Never yield to temptation, though it smile at you in the
social home glass. Never have your own wife raise the first glass to
your trembling lips. Nonsense! I'm no temperance quack. What
good will it do you to join these Good Templars?

CHARLIE. I believe in unity there is strength, and wish to surround
myself with temperance friends, who will, by their example and influence, shield me from that temptation to which we are all too apt
to yield; and then, if I am sick, I have brothers and sisters to watch
over me in kindness or bury me with real regard.

FRANK (*looking at glass*). Well, now, I am opposed to these Good
Templars—always have been. When I was a teetotaler, six months
ago (*looks at bottle*), I said there was no danger of my ever becoming a drunkard. (*Reaches across* CHARLIE's *lap to seize glass with
right hand.*)

CHARLIE (*grasping hand, raises it up, and looks squarely into*
FRANK's *face*). Do you think so now?

FRANK. (*After pause, sighs.*) Well, that's a little mixed; but I
don't believe these Good Templars ever save the moderate in-
dulger.

CHARLIE. (*Rises and puts chair back.*) I know they do; and, better still, they save the young from becoming such. If drunkards are only moderate drinkers fully developed, and this society can save the men and women—

FRANK. (*Rises quickly.*) That's right, my covey, put in the women. My wife was a woman.

CHARLIE. Your poor wife is now a noble-hearted woman, and has joined this order, knowing how powerful is woman's influence for good or evil. Her experience has made a true-hearted woman from a false-headed girl.

FRANK. (*Moves chair back.*) All right, Charlie, join these secret plotters against our liberties. Good-by. (*As* CHARLIE *starts out* C.) Stop! (*Gets bottle and glass. Fills it.*) Six months ago, you urged me to drink a certain toast. Allow me to return the compliment. (*Gives* CHARLIE *glass, and fills another from table* R.) To the Independent Order of Good Templars. May they save us all from becoming drunkards. (FRANK *drinks.* CHARLIE *stands without drinking. Closed in.*)

SCENE II.—*Music for song. Street or wood in front. At change, procession of Good Templars in full regalia come out, ladies* L. 1 E., *forming across stage in front. Gentlemen enter* R. 1 E., *and form in rear. They sing some popular temperance glee or Templar's ode, and then ladies exit* R. 1 E., *and at same time gentlemen exit* L. 1 E. *Change scene.*

SCENE III.—*Lively music at change. Full stage, with elegant counter at back, upon which is display of bottles, glasses, etc. Small card-tables, with flowers upon them,* R. *and* L. *Pistol, sure fire, behind bar, where* BENTON *is discovered.*

FRED. (*Enters* L. 1 E.) Aw, Wichawd, how long befoah the masquewade commences?

DICK. Only a few moments, Mr. Rawlings. Will you join them?

FRED. Perhaps. Give me some bwandy.

DICK. Certainly, sir. You had better join the masqueraders. A lot of strange ladies present to-night.

FRED. Aw! Well, I'll see who they awe, as I only wish to associate with wespectable society, you know—eh? Wichawd? (*poking* DICK *in ribs.*) By the way, I heard that the women's committee on saloon pwayeh-meetings called to see you to-day.

DICK. Yes, they wanted to hold a religious service here to-night. I told them my license did n't specify that kind of business, and I should not admit them. Fact is, I'm more afraid of this religious women's war on whisky than of all the laws on the statute-books. (FRED, *having drunk, starts away.*) Let me see, did you pay for that?

FRED. Weally, these women made me fohget to pay the dime.

DICK. Dime nothing. Twenty cents.

FRED. Watheh high-toned, by jove!

DICK. Why, confound your impudence, do you take this for a ten-cent chebang?

FRED. Aw, no. It's moah demnable. It's a high-pwessuah concert saloon. (*Sits at table* R. *Shuffles cards.*)

FRANK. (*Enters* L. 1 E.) Halloo! Richard's himself again!

DICK. And Raymond is a *man*. (*They shake hands.*)

FRANK. Thank you. Just heard that you have a gay old place here. Female masqueraders—eh? you rascal? You see I'm pretty well posted, if I have just returned from abroad.

DICK. How's your excellent wife?

JOE *enters* L. 1 E.

FRANK. O, quite womanly, thank you.

JOE. (*Crosses to* FRANK.) Yes, Massa Frank, and dat be why she am now cryin' an' takin' on so awful, 'cos you dun gone off down here and leab her all alone. Now, massa, I ain't 'tickler 'bout de kind ob company I keep, 'cos I'se only a black nigga; so you just leab me here to drink de licker wid dese galoots, an' you go home an' s'prise Miss Allie.

FRANK. (*Throws him aside.*) O, get out, you black rascal! (*All laugh.*)

JOE. O, you need n't laugh, white folks. Mas'r Frank nebber calls ole Joe black rascal 'cept when he's in dis kind ob a crowd. (*Exit* . 1 E.)

L FRANK. I say, Dick, do you remember the muss we had up at that picnic, when you threatened to pour a glass of liquor down my throat? Ha! ha! ha! Just try me now. (*Leans over counter.*) O, was n't I jolly green?

JOSH *enters* L. 1 E.

JOSH. Yes, and now you're jolly dry. Look out for spontaneous combustion, or you'll burn up, one of these days.

FRANK. And Josh, too. I declare, you look spruce. (*They shake hands.*)

JOSH. Yaas, and you look kinder dandyish since you returned from Europe.

FRANK. Come up to the rack and nominate your pizen.

JOSH. Whisky straight. If I am bar-tender, I'll drink with an old friend.

FRED. (*Jumps up quickly.*) Cowwect! So will I, by jingo!

DICK *fills glasses.*

FRANK. I declare, Fred, I did not recognize you. (*They shake hands.*) What is your best hold?

FRED. Aw, Wichawd, as usual, high-toned—(*aside*) when I'm tweated.

FRANK. You, too, Dick. Swallow your own bitter pills. (*They all click glasses and drink.* JOSH *passes behind bar.*) Halloo, Josh, you appear at home. (*Goes to table* R., *and plays with* FRED.)

DICK *exits* R. U. E.

JOSH. Yaas, I'm now Mister Benton's head clerk. Beats creation how it raises one in public estimation to stand behind a whisky-bar out West here. Now, in Varmount, where they're all so pesky old-fashioned, somehow they don't look up to a bar-tender. He can't go in good society. Out here, if a man keeps a whisky-shop, he is quite respectable. If he is fortunate enough to own a wholesale liquor-store, he belongs tew the *aristocracy;* and if he runs a distill-ery, his ring will be pretty sure tew send him tew Washington tew watch our legislation. O, I know the ropes. I'm getting tew be quite a politician myself. (*Drinks a big swallow, and chokes.*) Fact, if bad whisky does kinder stagger me a little. I'm going to run for Sheriff of —— County. I'm not Josh any more. I'm *Mister* Slender. I goes in good society, because—well, because I wear good cloaths, and because—because I do.

DICK enters R. U. E.

DICK. The lady masqueraders will now enter. (*The ladies enter* R. *and* L. U. E., *and form up and down stage. They all wear masks.*) Select your partners for a quadrille.

Dance-music heard at back. Just as sets are forming, ladies throw off masks. Music stops as ladies sing, "COME, YE SINNERS, POOR AND NEEDY." FRANK *and* FRED *at table back, quietly playing cards.* DICK, *with bowed head, behind counter. At end of third verse,* FRANK *jumps up.*

FRANK. That's not fair.
FRED. You cheated. You did, by jove! (*Rises slowly.*)
FRANK. You lie! (*Draws pistol.* FRED *draws knife.* DICK *leaps upon counter.*)
DICK. Stand back there, you rascal!

He fires at TOM FRAZIER, *who has rushed between* FRED *and* FRANK. *He falls dead* C. *Other characters take attitude of horror. Police-man enters* L. U. E. *Shakes club at* DICK. *Ladies all kneel, as though in silent prayer, keeping* C. *of stage open, to show audience man lying on stage. Scene changes to slow, plaintive music.*

SCENE III.—*Wood or street, front.*

JOSH. (*Enters* L. 1 E., *running and drunk.*) Consarn these Meth-odists! Jingo! I forgot that my old mother belonged tew that persuasion. I'll take that cuss-word back for her sake. Where in Sam Hill are all the perlice? They are allus a little too late. If I'm ever killed when I'm drunk—no, I mean when I'm sober, for I'm never drunk—hic. If I'm ever killed, drunk or sober, I'll never pay another doggoned cent city taxes. Now, I've hearn tell that when a man is half-tight he generally speaks the truth; and, as I'm 'bout half-way—hic—fashionable, I hope, if Dick hears me, he'll lay it tew the whisky; but, by the jumpin' jehosiphat, I don't believe it is right tew sell men any thing that makes 'em act the way they dew at the Gem every night. Chaw me inter fine-cut terbacker if I b'lieve sellin' licker is half as respectable as organ-grindin' with a lame monkey, and drinkin' licker is a cussed sight worse. How in blue blazes has drinkin' licker improved Frank Raymond? I kinder 'bout half believe that old-fashioned mother of mine was just about half right when she sed tew me, sed she, "Josh, Joshua my son, Josephus, licker is cussed, and any man that sells it is a—

DICK enters R. 1 E.

DICK. Josh!

JOSH. Is a gentleman.

DICK. Why did you leave the saloon?

JOSH. Thought I saw old Van Pelt's ghost—

DICK. Why did you run?

JOSH. Did I run?

DICK. Did you run? Well, I should think you did.

JOSH. Wall, I rather thought so myself, but I was n't quite sure.

DICK. Were you afraid of the dead man?

JOSH. No, but I was of them live fellers, pullin' out their knives an' pistols. They were masked; and, if I'd been killed, how in thunder would I have known who to lick for it? Dick, I do n't like the concert business. I hain't got a good ear for its music. I do n't object tew the shootin', but somehow that hymn that my old-fashioned mother used tew sing hit me mighty hard right here. (<i>Hits left breast.</i>) If you've no objections, I'll resign and go into a lower grade of business—turn politician.

DICK. Then I suppose you'll not object to learn that these Good Templars have organized this woman's war on King Alcohol, which is being led by Dio Lewis?

JOSH. Bully for Dio (<i>dancing</i>)!

DICK. Curse him! (<i>Savagely.</i>)

JOSH. Yes, cuss him. (<i>Stops quickly.</i>)

DICK. They have, by their prayers and hymns, compelled me to vacate the Gem for a daily prayer-meeting.

JOSH. Jerusalem! Say, Dick, let's demoralize, and go to work like honest men—sawin' wood.

DICK. Work! No, thanks to my sharpness. I have leased, in a less fashionable locality, a common bar-room; and not all the Good Templars, women, or doctors this side of—(JOSH <i>stops him by gesture</i>)—hades shall drive me out. Come on. I will open it to-night, and need your help (<i>going</i>).

JOSH. But, I say, Dick, is a common whisky bar-room like ————'s respectable?

DICK. Respectable? Why, confound your impudence, do n't they have back doors? Do n't some of our moral reformers patronize them? Do n't two-thirds of our lawyers and doctors support them? Do n't our commissioners and city councils license them? Respectable? Ha! ha! ha! Yes, and fashionable, too. (<i>Exit</i> R. I E.)

JOSH. All right, DICK, I'll foller; for a man might as well be dead as out of fashion. If I ever catch old Lewis sneakin' 'round our back door, I'll pelt him. (<i>Exit</i> R. 1 E. <i>Change scene.</i>)

SCENE IV.—*Interior plain. Sewing-machine* C., MRS. LENA BOS-
WORTH *operating it. Table* L. C., *upon which lady is cutting out
patterns.* ELLA *fast asleep in big chair* L. FANNIE *sewing* R.
Enough other ladies to fill scene at work R. *and* L. *At change all
applaud.*

FANNIE. Ha! ha! ha! Lena Bosworth in favor of female suffrage.

LENA. Yes, I am in favor of female suffrage—not because I believe
it is our natural sphere; but, when I look about me and see how
women have to suffer from the corruption of political parties, I say
she should be allowed the privilege of exercising her right to use
the balance of power which her vote would command. She would
purify our political, as she does our social element of society. I say
she should be allowed at least this one weapon of elective franchise
to shield herself from unjust laws. (*Applause.*)

FANNIE. Really, Mrs. Bosworth, you ought to take the stump, and
turn female lecturer. (*All laugh.*)

LENA. My dear girl, you are unjust to meet my arguments, which
you can not answer, only with such silly ridicule. (*Applause.*)

FANNIE. Yes, but all the women would vote as their fathers, brothers, or husbands do.

LENA. Do you think, if the women of this city could vote, that
Dick Benton could renew his liquor-license?

ELLA. No, never! (*Rises quickly.*)

LENA. Be careful, Miss Ella. You are a trance-medium, and have
just delivered a wide-awake argument in favor of female suffrage.
(*All laugh.*)

ELLA. I am not asleep now. Any woman who would sleep when
this question is being discussed should sleep forever, and never wake
up to know her shame. I am not a woman's rights woman, because
I believe this same object can be accomplished outside the political
arena.

FANNIE. Well, Miss Wideawake, I should like to have you tell us
how.

ELLA. Let woman exert her influence at home; in the nurseries
where every childish ache is not dosed with a little sweetened
brandy; in the parlors where our young people shall not be intro-
duced to temptation.

LENA. At picnics where ladies do not drink wine. (*All laugh.*)

ELLA. The result of that day has taught us all a lesson; and I now
say, at our daily tables, in private and public, let the ladies, the true-
hearted women, educate public sentiment to discountenance the man-
ufacture, sale, or use, wholesale or retail, of spirituous liquors. Let
us all wake up to this great question of woman's influence. (*All
applaud, and* ELLA *falls asleep.*)

FANNIE. "Tired nature's sweet restorer, balmy sleep." Now, tell
me, Mrs. Bosworth—for you have lost your trance-medium—do you
believe women could do this?

LENA. From my heart of hearts, I believe she could. I believe
that, were every lady of —— to swear by the memory of the
wrongs intemperance has caused her sex; by the homes it has deso-

lated and grave-yards populated; by the widows it has made and the orphans bereft; by the ocean of blood and tears wrung from innocent hearts—let them swear by their purity, by their virtuous womanhood, that they will not associate, in private or public, with any man, be he friend or lover, who countenances the sale, wholesale or retail, or the use, allopathic or homeopathic, of intoxicating liquors, and—mark my word—before the next election-day in ——. woman's influence would stuff the ballot-box with temperance votes. (*All applaud.* ALLIE *speaks outside* L. 1 E.)

ALLIE. Lena! Lena! Pity! O, pity me!

LENA. What is it, darling? (ALLIE *enters* L. 1 E.)

ALLIE. O, Mrs. Bosworth! Frank, my husband, whom I tempted to drink the first glass, is being lured down to ruin by his evil genius, Dick Benton.

LENA. But his saloon has just been transferred to the Ladies' Anti-Saloon Society, where they will establish the head-quarters of their daily prayer-meetings.

ALLIE. I know that; but he immediately reopened his vile den on —— street. (O, would to Heaven that breathing-hole of infamy were purged by fire!) And even there, in his degradation, has Frank followed him. I have just been to Mr. Benton, and, upon my very knees prayed, as only a drunkard's wife can pray, that he would sell my husband no more liquor. He swears that his license for that bar continues an entire year, and not all the Good Templars or prayer-meetings in the universe shall stop his vile traffic.

LENA. O, Mrs. Raymond, I do pity you; Heaven alone knows how sincerely; but what can we women do against this giant evil?

ALLIE. In the first place, let every woman who hears me to-night remember by the example of my misfortune never to offer the first glass of temptation to man, woman, or child.

LENA. This will not assist you in rescuing your husband from a drunkard's grave.

FANNIE. O, I wish I was a man! (*Rises quickly. Her chair falls over.*)

ELLA. So do I. (*Yawns.*)

FANNIE. I'd march straight over to Dick Benton's bar-room, and would take him by the collar and say to him: Dick Benton, your bar-room is a nuisance to this community. It is the only alluring door-way to hell now open to our young men. You are sending our fathers, sons, brothers, lovers, and friends down to delirium and death. Now, sir, listen. Close up this bar-room in just three minutes, or I'll tumble your bar through your window and kick you into the street. (*All applaud.*)

ELLA. So would I. (*Yawns, and all laugh.*)

LENA. (*Rises.*) O, ladies! sisters! The thought, the desire of my heart, is wild, wicked, and reckless; but, if that bar-room was closed, Frank Raymond, your husband, our fathers, brothers, and friends, might be lured from the downward path to ruin. Will every one here present, who has some one who is near and dear to her heart, who is treading the path of desolation and death across Dick Benton's threshhold—will all such rise to their feet? (ALLIE, FANNIE, *and nearly all ladies rise.*) So many! O, so very many! Friends, this is infamous. This man Dick Benton is the destroyer of our once happy homes; his bar-room, our hell on earth. He is retailing our very heart's blood and bitter tears for gold, in his damnable traffic. Were it stopped! were his bar-room closed! Should it be destroyed? Do you wish the vengeance of a just God would descend upon it in a lightning-flash from heaven? If this fiend hardens his heart against woman's prayers and woman's tears, would you, my sisters, raise your arms and strike, to close his vile den forever?

ALL LADIES (*rising*). Yes! yes! forever!

LENA. Then place your hands above your wildly beating hearts, and swear (*they do so*): Swear by our hopes of peace here and happiness hereafter; swear by our love for those we seek to save; swear by our purity and our misery; swear by ourselves, that Dick Benton shall close at once and forever his bar-room, or we, his victims, will be our own avengers!

Ladies stand in tableau, as curtain falls slowly, with low, plaintive music. CURTAIN.

ACT III.

SCENE I.—*Dancing-music. Interior plain. Full stage. A common plain counter runs across stage at back. Behind this, and high enough to show from front, are two or three shelves, upon which are quantity of old bottles, etc. Upon counter are bottles, and glasses. An old table for cards stands* R. C. *A large empty barrel, with upper head out, stands* L. C., *with bucket of saw-dust behind it. Three beer-kegs stand* L. 2 E. *Whisky-barrel stands* R. 2 E. *A bench in front of counter, on which* JOE *lies asleep. Three or four drunken loafers at table. At curtain,* DICK *and* JOSH *take a drink behind counter, then come out.*

DICK. Come, now, boys, it's time to close up.

JOSH. Yes, we've got all their money.

DICK. All you drunken loafers ought to be at home. Get out!

DICK *and* JOSH *put men out* R. *and* L. JOSH *then goes and shakes* JOE, *who snores violently, when* JOSH *turns bench over.* JOE *rolls well down stage, and makes a hasty exit* L. 1 E., DICK *kicking him.*

DICK. Ah! come in, Mr. Raymond.

JOSH. Yes, he's got a little money left yet.

FRANK. (*Enters* L. 1 E., *very drunk. He has his hankerchief in his left hand.*) Say, fellers, seen any thing—hic—of my spogget-handkerchief? (*Coming up stage,* JOSH *steals it out of his hand.*)

JOSH. Yaas, Mister Raymond, I found it 'bout an hour ago, up there by the counter.

FRANK. Thank you—hic. There's a dollar for you. (*He puts handkerchief in pocket, gives* JOSH *dollar, and* DICK *steals handkerchief.*)

JOSH. As my old-fashioned marm used tew say, "Josh," sed she, "Joshua my son, Josephus, honesty is the best policy." (*Pockets dollar. Josh exits* R. 2 E.)

FRANK. Now, then, give me another—hic—drink; and I'll go home to my fife and wamily.

DICK. (*Steps behind counter.*) Another drink? Yes, sir. Certainly, sir. (*Fills tumbler.*) Ten cents.

FRANK. Correct. (*Goes to take it, but every time he does so, DICK puts his hand on glass.*)

DICK. Ten cents, sir.

FRANK. That's all right.

DICK. Ten cents, you rascal.

FRANK. Chalk it down.

DICK. Not much, Mary Ann.

FRANK. Well, I'll give me your note.

DICK. Cash down, you puppy!

FRANK. (*Pays it.*) You used to charge twenty cents at the Gem Saloon.

DICK. Yes; but, as we go down in the scale of respectability, things fall.

FRANK. So they do. (*He goes to drink quickly, and falls onto bench.*)

DICK. Want any more liquor?

FRANK. Not unless you've got a—hic—force-pump.

DICK. (*Comes out at him.*) Then get out of here. You ought to be ashamed to make such a beast of yourself. (*Pulls him down* C.) Come, get out. We want to shut up.

FRANK. Well, why do n't you shut up—hic.

ALLIE *enters* L. 1 E. DICK *releases* FRANK. *who staggers* R. *and sits in chair.*

FRANK. (*Aside.*) I should think my wife could get liquor enough for a woman Good Templar by smelling of my breath. (*Aloud.*) What do you want?

ALLIE. I desire Mr. Benton to promise not to sell you any more liquor.

FRANK. Well, he won't do it.

ALLIE *goes up to* DICK *and kneels.*

ALLIE. O, sir, are you human? How many times have I and other wives and mothers kneeled thus before you in disgraceful humility, and begged you not to sell those we love more liquor! Do not, O do not give Frank that which turns my love almost to hate. (*She gets up.*)

DICK. See here, woman, I have been tormented with you enough for one day; and, if you come here any more with your prayers and tears, I'll kick you out.

FRANK. You? you kick my wife? O, this cursed liquor! Has it made me such a stupid brute?

DICK. Now, madame, get out, or I'll—(*Raises bottle, as though to strike her.*)

FRANK. Look here, Dick Benton, 1 am not quite drunk enough to sit here and see my wife insulted by a dog like you. (*Jumps up and raises chair over* DICK's *head, who lowers bottle, and* FRANK *resumes seat.*)

DICK. Now, Frank, do n't get mad. You and I are too old friends to quarrel about a woman. Mrs. Raymond, if you are through, you had better skedaddle.

ALLIE. I am not through. I will usurp my very nature to accomplish the object of this dreaded visit. Will you promise to sell my husband no more liquor?

DICK. No. (*Goes behind bar.*)

ALLIE. Beware, Mr. Richard Benton. I hold your very life in my power. I warn you of the consequences to refuse. Your property is in danger. Now, sir, for the last time, will you continue to sell all our fathers, husbands, and sons liquor?

DICK. Here, Josh! (JOSH *enters* R. 2 E.) There 's going to be a row.

JOSH. With the women? O, Lord!

ALLIE. Will you sell liquor to my husband?

DICK. Just as long as he can stagger up to that bar and pay for it.

LENA. (*Enters* L. 1 E.) Then, sir, you must close this bar.

DICK. And who in thunder are you?

LENA (*advancing.* JOSH *retires behind counter.*) An honest woman.

DICK. O, yes, I know you now. You are one of these Good Templars. What do you want?

LENA. Nothing but God's justice.

DICK. I 'll have no praying in the saloon.

LENA. (*Aside.*) Then you 'll have a big row. (*Aloud.*) I ask you, in all kindness and Christian charity and forbearance, to read that paper. It 's a pledge not to sell Frank Raymond more liquor. (*She hands it to him.*)

DICK. And this is the use I make of it. (*Tears it up.*) Look here, madame, you cursed Good Templars, with your prayer-meeting, have made me vacate my Gem Saloon. You have scared off, prayed off, or bought off every saloon-keeper in ——; but there is my license, signed, sealed, and stamped. Do you doubt its legality?

FRANK (*staggering up to bar*). Le' me see it, Dick.

DICK. Yes, read it, Mr. Raymond. I know you are a lawyer.

FRANK. You should n't judge by appearances—hic.

DICK. Is it not legal?

FRANK. No, I think not. (*Tears it up.*)

DICK. Scoundrel, I 'll have you arrested for this crime.

FRANK. Crime? O, I 'm too—hic—drunk to be responsible.

DICK. Well, license or no license, you shall neither sing nor pray here. Neither will I refuse to sell this fool liquor, nor will I close this bar.

LENA. Then Richard Benton, we will—

DICK. We? Who?

LENA. The avengers.

Ladies step out from all entrances, with hatchets and axes raised. Stand a moment in tableau. Then DICK *seizes hatchet from behind counter.* JOSH *falls behind counter.* FRANK *rises from chair.*

DICK. Death and furies! The first woman who lays hands on my property dies! (*Raises hatchet.*)

FRANK. (*Draws and presents pistol at* DICK.) Steady there, Dick Benton. I am just drunk enough to blow your infernal brains out, if you do n't kneel down and say your prayers.

Music by orchestra, "COME, YE SINNERS, POOR AND NEEDY." *As* DICK *kneels,* FANNIE *and* ALLIE *pull over counter.* JOSH *leaps out and jumps into barrel.* ELLA *pours saw-dust into it, and he stands up as though begging for mercy.* LENA *and a lady pull over shelving at back, while all other ladies are bursting up barrels and old furniture as curtain falls.* CURTAIN.

ACT IV.

Music, "FATHER, DEAR FATHER, COME HOME WITH ME NOW," *at curtain. Interior very poor. A bundle of straw* R. U. E., *with old blanket over it.* FRANK *lies on this, but does not sleep. During scene, he keeps moving about hands, points around stage, and is very uneasy.* ALLIE *sits upon low stool at his* L.

ALLIE. O, misery! misery! Great Heaven, is there no hope? Am I powerless to save the husband whom I have murdered—the husband who, but for my mad, girlish act in tempting him to drink the first glass of wine, might even now be my protector, instead of being dependent upon one who, in her weakness and poverty, is all powerless to save from the ravings of delirium? O, if he would only sleep! If not, he will die, and I shall be his murderer. O, how I keep wishing that the fashionable circle which surrounded us on our wedding-night could stand beside us now, and see the last sad, sad scene in the career of the poor drunkard! I wish all the great world of moderate drinkers, old and young, rich and poor, could see the drunkard's home. O, father!

JUDGE CUSHING *enters* L. 1 E. ALLIE *starts toward him.*

JUDGE. Stop! Is your husband dead?
ALLIE. No, thank Heaven!
JUDGE. Good morning. (*Going* L.)
ALLIE. Father, would you desert us again? Can you not forgive, even upon his death-bed, one whom you and I have assisted in laying there.
JUDGE. O, do n't preach to me. I am too nervous. I never wished him to be more than a social fellow well met. I never expected he would make a fool of himself this way. I do n't see why it is that some people can, and, as I know from experience, do drink all their lives, and yet only be moderate drunkards—ah, hem!—drinkers, (bless my soul, how nervous!) while others, in a few years, make perfect sots of themselves.

ALLIE. But, since so many, so very, very many do, let those who are only moderate drinkers be warned, fearfully warned, by the example of his misfortune.

JUDGE. There, there, that will do. I keep telling you I am too nervous to listen to your temperance lectures. Come, pack up your duds, if you've got any he has not pawned for liquor—pack up and come home again.

ALLIE. O, father, dear, good father, are you in earnest? Have you forgiven us? Will you, indeed, rescue us from this squalid misery?. Have you come to save us from starvation?

JUDGE. Now, now, don't get pathetic. Don't you hear me keep telling you I am nervous?

ALLIE. But tell me, do you think, are you sure it would be safe to remove Frank?

JUDGE. Remove Frank? Well, I rather think not.

ALLIE. O, thank you! I knew you would be mindful of Frank.

JUDGE. Yes, I will be mindful of Frank. You don't suppose I would take him back again now, after having kicked him out a year ago. You alone are welcome to return to a home he has disgraced.

ALLIE. But, Father, you certainly do not expect me to leave Frank?

JUDGE. Why not. Can Frank provide for you? Can Frank keep you from starving? Can Frank keep even this crazy old nervous roof above you much longer? Can Frank support you in his brandy? Tell me how many months ago was it that he turned you from this very door, and with kicks, cuffs and curses, ordered you to leave his home forever? I will send Joe over to watch until he is better. (*Dead.*) So you can come home to your former life of luxury.

ALLIE. But, Father.

JUDGE. Come, come, now, no nonsense; no nervousness. Choose quickly. Home with me to a life of happiness, or home here, and a death of misery.

ALLIE. You are cruel to doubt my choice. You have ever been a kind and indulgent father to me, and now offer me what—with starvation staring me in the face, it is hard, very hard, to refuse. I expect to die if I remain here; but in life or death, I am still Frank Raymond's wife.

JUDGE. You will stay—

ALLIE (*Goes to Frank.*) Where the wife's duty calls here forever.

JUDGE. Good bye. *Exit* L. I E.

ALLIE. Father, Father, one word; one kind word at parting. Father, Frank, Oh, Father. ALLIE *exits* L. I E.

FRANK. (*Raises upon elbow.*) Allie, Allie, don't go; don't leave me alone. (*Raises upon knee.*) Gone, gone. Oh, Heavens, come back to me, Allie; don't desert me while all these creeping rascals are about me, dropping from the ceiling onto my head. See, yonder in the corner; see it's eyes! hear it snap it's teeth! Yonder through the door, see that crawling snake, creeping this way, soft and gently gliding nearer. I'll run. (*He can't.*) No, no, I can't move. I can't escape. Oh, how it's glistning eyes bind me charmed by the serpent of the still. Now it's twining about my legs, twisting about my body, coiling around my throat. Help! help! Murder! (*Falls* c.)

(ALLIE *enters* L. 1 E. *Rushes to* FRAMK *and kneels.*) Oh, Frank, my husband. Lost, lost, forever. (*Drops head upon* FRANK's *breast. Closed in. Music repeats* FATHER, DEAR FATHER.)

SCENE II.—*Street, or wood front.*

DICK. (*Enters* L. 1 E.) Confound these Good Templars. They chase me like blood hounds. Well, let them howl. They have run me into my den, at last, and let them find me, if they can. First, their prayer meeting closed up my concert saloon, and I fell one step lower. Next, that mob of she devils gutted my bar-room, and I only got my fingers burned for sueing them. Next, I found a stand outside the city limits. Ah, ha, ha. There I had thwarted these praying Templars. Ha, ha, ha; but my shanty was struck by lighting, and down I tumbled another peg. Step by step have these advocates of temperance reform been yelping at my heels, until they have driven me into my underground doggery, where Frank Raymond and other such customers can't come to me. So I am going after my customers. (*Exit* R. 1 E.)

JOE *enters slyly* L. 1 E.

JOE. Yes, and there's still anodder hound dat's trackin' you like a roarin' lion, seekin' who he may dewour. Look out, Old Benton, dars a niggh roun' here somewhere. I smells him, suah. (*Exti* R. 1 E. *Change scene.*)

SCENE III.—*Interior of cellar. Full stage. Barrel stands* C. *with words* "*whiskee, 2 sents a swig,*" *chalked upon it. Wooden faucet for drawing liquor; quart cup under this.* JOSH *seated on barrel, with tin pint cup in his hand; it has a big stamp on bottom. Music at curtain,* "JOHNNIE, FILL UP THE BOWL."

JOSH. Wall, I wonder if selling liquor is respectable? I've 'bout made up my mind that my old fashioned marm was exactly right, when she sed tew me, Josh, sed she, Joshua, my son, Josephus, drinkin' licker is worse than suckin' hell-fire through a rye straw, and sellin' is as much worse as wholesalin' is worse than retailin'. (*Looking about stage.*) This don't look tew me as though it was either respectable, fashionable, or payin'. (*Looks at bottom of cup.*) That's a government stamp. Dick pays his duties on whisky as its drank, and that's why its tew cents a swig. Co's this one cent stamp does till the cup's eat up by the pesky stuff. (*Sits down.*) Beats all how all our fashionable customers have gone back on us unless like Frank Raymond, they have gone down with us. (*Draws licker.*) Durn the licker business. (*Drinks.*) This a nice place tew wind up our business for when Dick got into my debt one dollar and sixpence on back salary, and ten shillings borried capital, he took me in equal partner and pretty considerably he took me in, too, for I dew all the work, and he takes care of the sinkin' fund. (*Drinks.*) So we don't have much floatin' capital. (*Drinks.*) Ten foot under the side walk; wonder if we aint about as low down as human's ever git in this world. (*Pulls up trap door in floor.*) Private grave-yard for our worn out customers.

(DICK *appears upon ladder; ladder set in* L. U. E. *He has* FRANK *in his arms.*)

DICK. What are you doing now?

JOSH. Seeing if this trap ain't next door to hell.

DICK. Here, help me down with this load.

JOSH. (*Goes up stage.*) Why, it's Frank Raymond; going to bury him down the trap, like what you did Tom Frazier?

DICK. Hush; here, help him down.

JOSH. All right, boss. (*Dick drops* FRANK *while* JOSH *is pulling off his coat.*)

DICK. Clumsy booby.

JOSH. So he is, (*kicks* FRANK *as he lays on stage,*) unless he's dead, or drunk.

DICK. No he's nearly dead for the want of a drunk. He is dying for the want of brandy.

FRANK. (*Raising to elbow.*) Brandy, brandy, brandy.

JOSH. Just as natural as life.

DICK. We must doctor him up. This old whisky is good medicine.

JOSH. (*Draws a cup of liquor.*) Wall, now, I don't know about that. My old-fashioned marm used tew say tew me, Josh, sed she, Joshua, my son, Josephus, a drug store that retails or a doctor who prescribes liquor for a patient, ought tew be regularly licensed as dealers in intoxicating liquor. Here, take your benzine. (JOSH *holds cup under* FRANK'S *nose; he seizes it quickly and drinks.*)

JOSH. Gosh-a-shun, he snaps at it like a mad dog.

FRANK. Brandy, brandy; whisky, more, more. (*Throws away cup.*)

JOSH. See here, don't break up our furniture that way. (FRANK *grabs quart cup and drinks.*) See here, Frank Raymond, have you gone into the wholesale liquor trade, or is the wholesale liquor going into you? Here, that ain't been stamped; you are making altogether too free. (*Takes measure away from him.*)

DICK. Yes, pay for what you have drank, and then measure the rest.

FRANK. Only one more swallow; see, I am better now. (*Gets up on knees.*) See how it strengthens me; now I am a man again. (*Stands up.*) Oh, if you love me—

DICK. Yes, and we love our money, too.

FRANK. Money, money, haven't I paid you every cent?

JOSH. No, not every cent, Frank; my books won't quite balance. (*Turns around barrel and shows a lot of tally chalk marks upon it.*) Figures won't lie.

FRANK. Oh, I am penniless.

DICK. That's all gammon; you used to have squads of money.

FRANK. Yes, and then I had friends; I used to have a pleasant home; I used to have a good name; I used to have a great many things which I have lost.

JOSH. (*Aside.*) Say, Dick, I wonder if he lost them all at our counter, as he did his pocket handkercher.

FRANK. I will have more whisky to keep these howling demons from roasting me alive. Brandy, brandy. (*Fall c. in front of barrel with head down the stage.*)

JOSH. If we give away our liquor, how are we to pay our income tax? Say, Dick, let's stamp this whisky in bulk. (*Raises foot over* FRANK.) Let's investigate his finances. (*They kneel on each side of him, and pull his pants pockets inside out, then rise.*)

JOSH. Say Dick, you picked up a dead duck; he ain't worth a cuss.

DICK. Take him up and drop him into the gutter. (*Josh partially lifts him.*) Stop. (*He drops him.*) If we take him up he may smell us out, when those Good Templars are watching, and then the police would make a raid on our underground doggery.

JOSH. Wall, Dick, what's to be did?

DICK. (*Picks up an ax.*) Dead men tell no tales.

JOSH. Yes, but I say, Dick, hold on a minute, is murder respectable?

DICK. He ought to have died six weeks ago, when his money was all gone, we had no further use for him; besides it would be a great blessing to his poor wife, and save the city his funeral expenses. (*Raises ax.*)

JOSH. Thunder and lightning, Dick, don't be in such a bloody pucker. Say, you hadn't better have no witnesses tew this little game. So, I'll just pop up on the sidewalk, and watch these sneaking police. (*Exit up ladder.*)

DICK. All right. (*Raising ax, then stops and takes a drink.*) Now, then, I'll tap him on the head, and quiet him forever. (*As he raises ax to strike,* Policeman leaps from ladder with club. JOSH jumps down with revolver pointed at DICK.)

JOSH. Steady, there, as my old marm used tew say—

JOE. (*On ladder.*) Niggah on de wood pile, don't you hear him holler.

(*Music,* "ROGUES' MARCH." *Closed in.*)

SCENE IV.—*Front street. Charlie and Fred enter L. 1 E.*

CHARLIE. Will you join our lodge of Good Templars?

FRED. (*Who is in rags.*) Oh, I'm afraid I am too far gone to be reclaimed.

CHARLIE. No, my friend, one year ago I said the same thing; I had suffered two attacks of delirium tremens. In comparison with my condition then Frank Raymond is now a respectable man. I was literally taken from the gutter by Lena Bosworth; taken to her pleasant home, nursed into sobriety, and then initiated into —— Lodge, and since that night, I have never tasted a drop of intoxicating liquor.

FRED. You were fortunate; but they would never receive such as me into their pure society.

CHARLIE. Certainly they will.. That is the great principle of their reform, "make every man a brother." No matter how low you have sunk in the scale of human degradation, make an effort to save yourself, and they will outstretch their hands with the friendly Templar's grip to assist you.

FRED. You seem very confident of their ability to save the poor drunkard.

CHARLES. I have "*Faith.*"

FRED. And then you speak to me so cheerfully of the future.

CHARLIE. Because, I have "*Hope.*"

FRED. But I don't see why you should trouble yourself about a poor, degraded wretch, like me.

CHARLIE. Because, I have "*Charity.*" Oh, Mr. Rawlings, these are magic words. They are the motto of an organization which is to-day wielding a mighty power for temperance reform. Good-night. (*Going* R.) I will see you again, in a few moments, when we will go to the hall of——Lodge. "Cast your destinies with them, there you are safe, the destroyer can never enter there." Remember the Good Templar's motto, "Faith, Hope, and Charity." (*Exit* R. 1 E.)

FRANK *enters* L. 1 E. *hat in hand.*

FRANK. Charity, charity, only a few pennies for a hungry man.

FRED. My dear fellow, are you really in want of food?

FRANK. Yes, sir, I am starving for one sup of brandy. (*Looks up at Fred.*)

FRED. Great Heavens! it's Frank Raymond! (*Turns* R.) Oh, Munson! Munson! take me to your temperance lodge. (*Exit* R. 1 E.)

FRANK. Go, go, before it is too late; for you were the first who, upon my wedding night, tempted me to drink.

JUDGE *enters* L. I E.

FRANK. Charity, charity, only a few pennies to a starving man.

JUDGE. Yes, yes, poor fellow, you look half famished. Don't hang your head. You need not be ashamed to beg, if you are hungry. Hold up your head (*Drops money into his hat*) like——Frank Raymond.

FRANK. (*Throws money at his feet.*) Keep your money, Judge Cushing. You and yours have paid your per centage towards making Frank Raymond a drunkard.

JUDGE. Oh, don't preach to me. I am too nervous. If you won't take money, here is a bottle of brandy. (*Takes it from his pocket and hands it to* FRANK.) Now, the best thing you can do is, to drink your fill and die, which would save me the trouble of going to the Court House after my daughter's divorce. (*Exit* L. 1 E.)

FRANK. The last bottle, and the farewell drink. (*As he raises it to his lips,* LENA, *who has hastily entered* L. 1 E. *siezes bottle.*) Let go of that bottle! It's mine; Father Cushing bequeathed it to me as a parting gift. Let go! I say. Take off your hand, or I'll (*Raises his right hand to strike, when he sees who it is.*) Lena Bosworth, do not rob me of my liquor.

LENA. If not it will rob you of life, as it has already, of everything else which once made life happy.

FRANK. Oh, I know, but I must have one more drink; the flames of hell are raging in my breast.

LENA. Would you add fuel to the flames?

FRANK. Oh! pity! pity, and despise me, but I must have liquor.

LENA. No! not another drop!

FRANK. Do not tempt me, woman. I am not Frank Raymond, to-night. I am a madman, and for one drop of liquor, I would strike you dead. (*He releases his hold of bottle to strike. She throws bottle off* L. 1 E: *and folds her arms across her breast.*)

LENA. Now, Frank, strike.

FRANK. Lost! lost! forever! (*Drops on knees.*)

LENA. No, not lost, but you are standing upon the crumbling brink of a drunkard's grave.

FRANK. And you, too, have come to curse me.

LENA. No, but with Heaven's help, to save you.

FRANK. Too late! too late! There is no hope.

LENA. While there's life there's hope. Frank Raymond, think! Remember the past. Reflect how, as a boy, you knelt down beside a dead father, and promised a dying, Christian mother, that you would never touch, taste, or handle the poison which killed your father.

FRANK. Great Heavens! and this is how I have kept that oath. (*Weeps.*)

LENA. Frank! Frank! Let me call you by the name your mother loved, and believe, with me, that she is to-night, looking down from her starry home, in Heaven, weeping, hoping, praying, and expecting your reform.

FRANK. Too late! I am a *friendless* drunkard.

LENA. (*Lays her hand on his shoulder.*) Not friendless while I live; not friendless wherever a Good Templar stretches out a helping hand. Frank Raymond, rouse yourself; be a man, once more. Call upon your lost pride; your honor; your manhood, to assist you. Remember, Dick Benton's bar-room is closed forever.

FRANK. Thank God.

LENA. There is now no alluring doorway of temptation open in ———. Look up. (*He does so.*) Now have "Faith," Stand up. (*He does so.*) Now have "Hope," and to prove that I have "Charity," make an effort to be Frank Raymond again, and there is a Good Templar's hand to save you.

FRANK. (*Takes her hand.*) Oh, madam, these are the first words of Christian kindness I have heard for many a weary month. Others have said, poor Frank, drunken brute; how I pity and despise him. And these have been the words of Christian charity with which the so-called, moral reformers have attempted to accomplish a reformation only to be secured by such noble acts as this. You have roused the little slumbering spark of manhood in my breast, and with Allie's prayers, I might have been saved, but she, too, deserted me.

LENA. No, she has not deserted you. Such a suspicion wrongs

woman's nature; does injustice to woman's love.. Look yonder (R. I
E.) is my residence. Come, Frank, I will prepare Allie for this great
happiness. (*Exit* R. 1 E.)
., FRANK. Dare I hope, Oh, Mother! Mother! is it thy sainted
spirit whispers to my trembling soul! Allie! darling, wife! Save
me from temptation. (*Exit* R. 1 E.)

Change scene. Music, "HOME, SWEET HOME."

———

SCENE V.—*Full stage. From* C. *off* L. U. E. *are steps, leading onto
porch with railing in front. Leads back to door in flat* L. U. E.
Scene backed by garden.

JUDGE CUSHING. (*Enters, dancing,* L. 1 E.) Bravo! bravo! I have
Allie's precious document safe at last; and, with this in one hand
(*holds up paper*) and Frank's ruin in the other (*holds up bottle*), I
can cry—(*raises bottle to lips.* FRANK *enters* R. 1 E.) Damnation!
FRANK. O, Allie, darling wife, save me from temptation! (ALLIE
appears upon porch L. U. E.)
ALLIE. Husband! (*Starts across porch.*)
FRANK. Wife! (*Going up to steps.*)

LENA *enters* L. 1 E.

JUDGE. Divorced! (*Steps between them and holds up paper.* ALLIE
sinks back into LENA's *arms, and is assisted off* L. U. E. ALLIE *drops
handkerchief on railing near door.*)
FRANK. Stand aside, old man. No power on earth shall keep me
from the presence of my wife.
. JUDGE. Stand back, young man. This (*holds up bottle*) has ever
stood between you and happiness. (*He sets it on railing near steps*
c.). Pass that sentinel, and at this door I'll meet you with my daughter's divorce. (*Holds it above head, and exits* L. U. E.)
FRANK (*at* R. 1 E.) O, man! man! are you human, to place in the
very path over which I must pass to happiness my deadliest enemy!
Fill yonder porch with armed men, and I will not falter. Place upon
the very step a fuse-lit cannon, and I will face it. Uprear a mountain
in its place, and I'll climb to her I love; but, as you love your soul's
eternal rest, hurl down that fiend incarnate! Allie! Allie! I come!
(*Staggers back.*) Death and destruction! The fumes of liquor send
me cowering back. (*Retreats to* L. 1 E.) Allie! Lena! I'll reach
your side, or fall beneath that bottle's power. (*He goes up left, and
finds* ALLIE's *handkerchief as his hand rests on railing.*) It's Allie's,
thank Heaven! (*Kisses it.*) Now, then, my precious one, I'll face
the dreaded foe. (*He covers face with handkerchief; but, as he gets
to bottle, his hand strikes it. He pulls off handkerchief, and raises
bottle to drink.*) Farewell, Allie! a long, a last farewell!
ALLIE (*from off stage* L. U. E.) O, Frank! Frank, my husband!.
(FRANK *does not drink, but puts bottle back on railing, and drops
down below porch, watching.*)

JUDGE. (*Enters* L. U. E.) I tell you he is not your husband, for I hold in my hand the court's decree of divorce.

ALLIE. (*Enters* L. U. E.) Whom God hath joined together, let not man put asunder. (LENA *enters* L. U. E. *All of them on porch.* ALLIE *takes divorce from* JUDGE.) This is man's decree of injustice (*tears it*), torn into fragments by woman's justice, and scattered to the winds of heaven by the breath of woman's scorn. (*As she throws scraps of paper over the railing, they fall like snow upon* FRANK, *who is kneeling below, porch being about four feet above stage.*) I tell you that in the sight of God I am still Frank Raymond's wife; and, though he is a hopeless drunkard, heart and soul, I love him.

JUDGE. (*Aside.*) Confound these women! They always make me nervous. (*Aloud.*) Very well, you are sealing your own doom. You are linking your future life with that of a miserable sot; for I tell you that, with that black bottle before him, Frank Raymond—

FRANK. (*Stands up.*) Would rise up, and, in the strength of his lost manhood regained, would seize the tyrant by his neck (*He seizes bottle.* JUDGE *rubs his hands with glee.* ALLIE *stretches hers out to* FRANK *imploringly.* LENA *raises hers in prayer*), and, by God's grace, dash it down to hell! (*He smashes bottle off* L. 2 E.)

ALLIE. Husband! (*She rushes into his arms.*)

FRANK. Wife! (*Kisses her.*)

JUDGE. Foiled! O, my nerves! (*Exit* R. 2 E.)

FRANK. Mrs. Bosworth, Allie, mother (*kneels*), hear my prayer, and register my oath in thy prayerful memory. Heaven giving me strength, and the Good Templars a home, I'll live or die a sober man!

ALLIE's *head on* LENA's *shoulder, with hand on* FRANK's *head.*

LENA. SAVED, THANK HEAVEN!

CHARLES MUNSON *enters* R. U. E., *leading* FRED RAWLINGS *by the hand, followed by* JOSH. *A* WORTHY CHIEF TEMPLAR *comes out from* L. U. E., *followed by other officers. Members of the order come on from* L. 2 E., *and all stand in tableau as slow curtain falls. Music,* "THE DOXOLOGY."

FINIS.

CPSIA information can be obtained
at www.ICGtesting.com
Printed in the USA
BVHW051109250219
541084BV00011B/1337/P